Inspired 2 Inspire

Walter "Walt-Leon" Davis Jr.

4-U-Nique
Publishing

Breaking the Status Quo, One Book at a Time.™

4-U-Nique Publishing
A Series of VLB/VBJ Enterprises, LLC

Inspired 2 Inspire

4-U-Nique Publishing books may be purchased for educational,
business, or sales promotional use. For information, please email:
info@4-U-Nique Publishing.com

First Edition

Cover Design By: 4-U-Nique Publishing

Library of Congress Cataloging-in-Publication Data

ISBN-13: 978-0-692-04122-2

ISBN-10: 0-692-04122-2

Table of Contents

APPRECIATION 1

BE THE EXAMPLE 3

BUILD YOUR TEAM 5

CHECK YOUR TEAM 7

CONTROL 9

DIAMOND 11

EXERCISE..13

FOCUS 15

GET OUT OF THE WAY 17

GROWTH 19

HAPPINESS 21

IT'S PART OF YOUR PROCESS 23

JOY 25

NOTHING IS IMPOSSIBLE 27

PASS THE TEST...29

PERSPECTIVE 31

POSITIVE..33

POWER..35

PURPOSE 37

REFLECT 39

REFOCUS..41

START NOW 43

STOP COMPLAINING 45

SUCCESS 47

THINK BEFORE COMPLAINING......................49

TIME FOR A CHANGE...51

TURN YOUR FEAR INTO FAITH 53

4-U-Nique Publishing..55

APPRECIATION

Take the time to appreciate where you are! Even though you're not where you want to be. Be appreciative of the fact that you're not where you used to be. When you stop complaining about where you are, you will realize that you are not as bad off as you think you are. If all you do is focus on where you are not, you will never get to where you want to be. You will never know your progress if you only focus on your setbacks.

SHOW APPRECIATION!

Be Great. Be Blessed. See A Life. Touch A Life. Change A Life!

BE THE EXAMPLE

You know why strangers support you more than the people you know? It is because the people who know you have a tough time accepting that they come from the same place as you and you are on a journey to do extraordinary things while they are not making any positive changes in their lives.

Do not let the talk of others about you of who you used to be, pull you back to where you've worked so hard to get away from. Whenever you feel a negative pull, think K.I.M (Keep It Moving)! Keep pressing forward. Do not allow anyone to make you feel bad because you are working hard to make a better life for yourself. Be the motivation and inspiration for others who want to get out of the place that they feel they are stuck in.

You never know who is watching you. Be The Example and show them that all things are possible (Philippians 4:13)

3

Be Great. Be Blessed. See A Life. Touch A Life. Change A Life!

BUILD YOUR TEAM

Build a team of people who have the same goals as you. Surround yourself with like-minded people. If you show me the five people you spend most of your time with, I can show you your future. If you are going to become successful in anything it wouldn't be wise to hang around people who want to be mediocre. Surround yourself with people that can match your ambition and push you to be better. Stay away from those who are comfortable with barely making it. Build Your Team of people that you know want "*it*" just as bad as you!

Be Great. Be Blessed. See A Life. Touch A Life.
Change A Life!

CHECK YOUR TEAM

Is everybody who you have around you really supporting you? Don't get so caught up in worrying if they are going to say you changed. You're supposed to change for the better. If people are trying to hold you back then you need to remove them from your life so they can no longer prevent your growth.

Be Great. Be Blessed. See A Life. Touch A Life. Change A Life!

CONTROL

Whenever you are doing something positive or trying to change for the better you will be tested. Something will happen or someone will attempt to pull you out of character and distract you from what you should be focused on. Don't allow anyone to have control over you. Don't let someone else move you from your place of peace and focus. Be positive. You are in charge of your actions, emotions, and reactions. YOU control YOU!

Be Great. Be Blessed. See A Life. Touch A Life. Change A Life!

DIAMOND

If you are going through a hard time in your life, stop complaining and be thankful for the process. To make a diamond you must apply pressure! As pressure is applied to your life, don't give up and let it be in vain. Go through the process and become the diamond that God has created you to be.

Be Great. Be Blessed. See A Life. Touch A Life. Change A Life!

EXERCISE

"Don't allow your gift to make you obese"- Lesley
Francisco McClendon

Exercise Your Gift! A good friend of mine named
Minister Lesley Francisco McClendon said, "its just like
when you're eating food. If all you do is eat and take in
food, but don't exercise, you will be obese, so if you just
hold that gift in you will become obese with dreams that
you will never get out!"

Exercise your gift and do what you love to do

Be Great. Be Blessed. See A Life. Touch A Life. Change
A Life!

FOCUS

WHAT ARE YOU SPEAKING OVER YOUR LIFE?

The power of life and death is in the tongue (Proverbs 18:20-21). You have the power to speak things into existence. If you speak positively, you will get positive results. For example: If you focus on being able to accomplish something, your actions will change and you will keep trying until you accomplish your goal.

Stop settling and stop complaining. Stay focused and stay true to what you ask for, and wait for God to give you what you were promised.

Be Great. Be Blessed. See A Life, Touch A Life, Change A Life!

GET OUT OF THE WAY

If you're sick and tired of your situation, sit back and allow God to do his job. While you're trying to get revenge on someone or fix a situation yourself, everything is getting worse and you're stressing over something that you have no control over. If you notice a bad situation is getting worse, it's probably because you're trying to do a job that's not yours to do. Get out of the way, sit back and allow God to do his job.

**Be Great. Be Blessed! See A Life. Touch A Life.
Change A Life!**

GROWTH

Life is about Growth! Don't get comfortable where you are and become stagnant. Continue to push yourself and reach for higher heights. The hunger you have when you first start off is the same hunger you should have after making a million dollars.

I remind myself about my growth every day. From recording my music in garages and bedrooms to now recording music in actual studios. From performing in front of 13 people at local events to now performing in front of thousands, across the U.S. This continuous growth is motivation to not stop and go backward but to keep striving for greatness and growing to where I want to be and most importantly where I need to be.

When you feel like you're stuck and don't know how or if you will ever get out of what you're going through, remember the times when you overcame you past struggles. It is all a part of the growing process!

Be Great. Be Blessed! See A Life. Touch A Life. Change A Life!

HAPPINESS

If Making You Happy Costs Me My Happiness, I Can't Afford You!

Look at the people around you. Are you always complaining about them? Are they making you better or slowing you down? Do you get positive vibes from them or negative energy? If they are not making you better, making you happy, helping you strive for greatness, or if they are even costing you your happiness than you may want to make some changes. Represent yourself and your family well.

Be Great. Be Blessed. See A Life. Touch A Life. Change A Life!

IT'S PART OF YOUR PROCESS

Don't be upset because you aren't where you want to be. Be thankful that you haven't become comfortable and you continue to work hard to better yourself and you situation. Until you give up, where you are is only temporary. It's just one step in your process toward success and greatness!

Be Great Be Blessed. See A Life. Touch A Life. Change A Life!

JOY

When people or the world starts to frustrate you, find Joy from deep within! That is true happiness. No one can steal your joy unless you let them. Don't give people or situations power over your happiness. Focus on God and you will find true Joy (John15:11).

Be Great. Be Blessed. See A Life. Touch A Life. Change A Life!

NOTHING IS IMPOSSIBLE

When the world tells you, "no, you're not qualified, you are too small, or it's impossible", God will tell you, "I gave you the vision and the dream, so I qualified you." God will put the perfect person in front of you to guide you to where you need to be. People will say it is impossible because it is impossible for them, but what God has for you is for YOU. Many of people called British inventor Humphry Davy crazy before he went on to invent the first light bulb in 1801. There were other people who worked on making the light bulb work effectively for everyday use. Thomas Edison made an effective light bulb in 1878 and filed for the patent in 1879. Thus proving that, because it is impossible for someone else does not make it impossible for you.

Sometimes God's answer is no to what you want because he has something better in store for you. Sometimes the answer is not yet because you're not ready yet, but NOTHING IS IMPOSSIBLE. In the words of the great poet, Matthew "Levi" St. Clair, "impossibility is the only impossibility because with God any and all things are possible."

Be Great. Be Blessed. See A Life. Touch A Life.
Change A Life!

PASS THE TEST

Often you ask, "why does God allow me to go through this" or "why does everything keep hitting me back to back?" You must realize that this is a test and you must pass.

Passing this test will start with transforming your mind. Don't sit around being sad and down because you're going through a challenge. Instead of focusing on what you're going through, you must realize that whatever you're going through you have already been prepared for. Settle down and think about the solution to the problem or the outcome you would like to get out of it. You may also say, "I prayed and asked God to fix it but he still let me go through it." THIS IS A TEST! The teacher is always quiet during a test. The teacher already prepared you with the necessary information to pass the test. Remember, God is the teacher.

Don't be discouraged. Recognize that you have the necessary tools that are required to pass the test. No more being a victim!

Be Great. Be Blessed. See A Life. Touch A Life. Change A Life!

PERSPECTIVE

Change your perspective and the outcome will change. If all you see is the negative in a situation, all you're going to get out of it is negative. How about trying, "Thank God I made it out of the last issue so I know I can make it out of this one too." Change your perspective from what you're going through to how you will get through. While you're busy focusing on what you're going through or what you've been through, you fail to realize the blessing of YOU'RE ALREADY THROUGH IT and no longer in it. You don't realize that every test that comes your way you were prepared for.

Now change your perspective and focus on what you want the outcome to be and not the situation that you're in. The more time you spend focusing on the outcome and seeing the positive, the less time you'll have to focus on the negative!

Your perspective can block your blessings and your destiny!

Be Great. Be Blessed. See A Life. Touch A Life. Change A Life!

POSITIVE

Don't complain because you're not where you want to be. Remember you're not where you used to be. If the door wasn't open for you, don't complain. Instead, thank God that you made it to where you are today.

It's a process. When you come from being unemployed, you celebrate becoming an employee and enjoy the journey of learning everything along the way and once you're prepared, you get a promotion. Be Positive! Why would God bless you with more if you can't appreciate what you have? Why would he bless you with the whole, if you can't manage the half?

Be Great. Be Blessed. See A Life. Touch A Life. Change A Life!

POWER

"YOU ARE A THREAT TO SATAN'S AGENDA"
- Pastor Lance Watson.

You have the power to tell Satan, "no" and destroy everything he is trying to do to you (Matthew 4:10). We will no longer allow him to have his way. We will no longer give up on ourselves. It is time for us to get back what God promised us and stop robbing ourselves. When you rob yourself that is Satan's plan working to perfection. Stop helping him and help yourself.

Be Great. Be Blessed. See A Life. Touch A Life. Change A Life!

PURPOSE

God didn't wake you up to complain, sit around and wait. He woke you up because he still has a purpose for your life. Today, live and move as if you have a mission to accomplish and purpose to fulfill. DON'T QUIT! KEEP PRESSING!

Be Great. Be Blessed. See A Life. Touch A Life. Change A Life!

REFLECT

Reflect on your past and be thankful for how far you have come. Appreciate the moment that you are living in and make the best of it. One day you will reflect back on what is now the present and you will be thankful for the lessons that you are currently learning. Don't rush the process. Enjoy the journey and pay attention along the way. Every step of your journey is a lesson learned and something to reflect back on later in life. Enjoy life and smile!

Today is the tomorrow you worried about yesterday. Well...YOU MADE IT!

Be Great. Be Blessed. See A Life. Touch A Life. Change A Life!

REFOCUS

Distractions will come your way. Distractions may come in the form family, friends, money, etc. The same way that God knows what you like, Satan also knows what you like. Satan knows what it will take to get you to focus on something other than what you need to focus on.

Remain focused and remember why you started out on this journey. This way you will never lose your drive or hunger. You will always be attentive and ready to accomplish the goals you have in mind.

Be Great. Be Blessed. See A Life. Touch A Life. Change A Life!

START NOW

We all have dreams. Do not keep pushing your dreams off by saying, "I'm going to start tomorrow" START NOW! Everyone isn't going to agree with you, but as long as you believe in yourself that's all that matters. People will see your passion and will believe in you sooner or later.

The NBA fined Michael Jordan $5,000 per game throughout an 82 game season for wearing a sneaker that he believed in. That is roughly $410,000 in fines when he only made $630,000 at the time. The NBA couldn't see how the sneakers were a fit for their league. Because Michael Jordan believed in something, the shoes and didn't give up, he helped inspire and build a brand. He is now a billionaire because of the brand he created that started with a simple sneaker.

GET OUT AND START NOW!

Be Great. Be Blessed. See A Life. Touch A Life. Change A Life!

STOP COMPLAINING

Instead of complaining about your situation and getting the same results over and over again, try being thankful that God knows you are strong enough to make it through that situation and he trusts you enough to handle it properly and not break. Be appreciative that God thinks enough of you that he keeps giving you trials to build you up and make you stronger. Once you transform your mind, you transform your results!

Be Great. Be Blessed. See A Life. Touch A Life. Change A Life!

SUCCESS

Success is not always what you see.

Stop comparing your success to someone else's success. If you continue to go down that path, you will never have enough in your eyes and you will never realize that you are already successful. Your definition of success may be different, so while you're so busy trying to keep up with what everyone around you has going on, you forget to pay attention to your journey, your purpose in life and you miss out on what success may be for you! Be yourself and focus on your life's calling, so you can have the success that is meant for you. You wouldn't know what to do with my success, and nobody in the world will know what to do with yours because it was meant for only you.

Be Great. Be Blessed. See A Life. Touch A Life. Change A Life!

THINK BEFORE COMPLAINING

Before you complain about where you are in your life, think about what you've been through and where you've come from. It's almost guaranteed that you will smile and realize you have nothing to complain about. Once you think about it and realize that you've come a long way, you will also remember that where you are is only a part of the process to get to where you want to be in life. Appreciate the little things you have now. If you stop and think about it, what you have now is the more you were once praying for!

Be Great. Be Blessed. See A Life. Touch A Life. Change A Life!

TIME FOR A CHANGE

When are you going to stop complaining about your situation and make the change you need to make a better YOU?

You complain about your job, but have you worked on your resume or qualifications required for you to get a better job? You complain about your weight, but are you still eating fast food all the time? You complain about your finances, but are you going out to eat often? Going out to the club or the bar with friends? Doing unnecessary shopping? Have you complained about being stuck in life, but still hanging out with the same people that aren't doing anything to better their lives?

It's time to stop complaining and look at yourself to see what changes you can make in order for your circumstances to change! You may have to cut off friends that you've had for years. You may have to give up doing something that you do all the time as a small step in your new direction. Example, if you go to the store every day

51

and buy a \$1 Arizona Tea, multiplied times 365 days per year, that's \$365 that you could have saved.

Look within yourself and pay close attention to your habits and see what you can change in order for your circumstances to change. What are you willing to sacrifice in order to stop complaining and make changes? IT'S TIME FOR A CHANGE!

Be Great. Be Blessed. See A Life. Touch A Life Change A Life!

TURN YOUR FEAR INTO FAITH

Don't let fear stop you from living your dream! With faith your chances are higher. With fear you have no chance. If you get past your fears and try, there is a chance that your dreams will come true. There's a chance that God will say no to what you want because he has something better for you. If you let fear hold you back, there is absolutely NO chance of your dreams becoming reality. Always remember that 50/50 is better than 0!

Be Great. Be Blessed. See A Life. Touch A Life. Change A Life!

4-U-Nique Publishing

Read excerpts, get exclusive inside looks at exciting new titles and authors, find tour schedules and enter contests.

www.4-U-NiquePublishing.com

Need help publishing your masterpiece? We are happy to help.

Email us at info@4-U-NiquePublishing.com

www.ingramcontent.com/pod-product-compliance
Lightning Source LLC
Chambersburg PA
CBHW021224020426
42331CB00003B/460